BECOME YOURSELF

A SELF-HELP ADULT COLORING BOOK
FOR RELAXATION & PERSONAL GROWTH!

60 CALMING DESIGNS TO COLOR!
FLOWERS & NATURE
ANIMALS
MANDALAS
DOODLES & PATTERNS

COLOR YOUR WAY TO A LIFE YOU LOVE™: BECOME YOURSELF

For information:
shellijohnson.com
alphadollmedia.com

Copyright Notice and Disclaimers

This book is Copyright © 2018 Shelli Johnson (the "Author"). All Rights Reserved. Published in the United States of America. The legal notices, disclosures, and disclaimers within this book are copyrighted by the Internet Attorneys Association LLC and licensed for use by the Author in this book. All rights reserved.

No part of this book may be reproduced or transmitted in any form or by any means, electronic or mechanical, including photocopying, recording, or by an information storage and retrieval system — except by a reviewer who may quote brief passages in a review to be printed in a magazine, newspaper, blog, or website — without permission in writing from the Author. For information, please contact the Author at the following website address: shellijohnson.com/contact

For more information, please read the "Disclosures and Disclaimers" section at the end of this book.

First Paperback Print Edition, June 2018

Published by Alpha Doll Media, LLC (the "Publisher").

ISBN: 978-1-948103-90-9

WELCOME TO THE
COLOR YOUR WAY TO A LIFE YOU LOVE™
COLORING BOOK SERIES!

AVAILABLE NOW OR COMING SOON!

UNLEASH YOUR INNER CREATOR & MAKE IT YOUR OWN!

This is not just another coloring book, it's also an invitation for you to delve deeper into who you are so you can find out what makes you come alive. I'm a big believer in the power of taking small steps to get you anywhere you need or want to go. With that in mind, I invite you inside these pages on a creative self-help adventure. You'll unleash your artistic side with designs and patterns while you do daily small-sized activities aimed at: 1. helping you heal yourself and 2. inspiring you to create a life you love. My hope is that you'll use these pages to ignite your imagination, discard your limitations, and free your inner creator.

Feel free to add your own personal embellishments to any image. You can make each page as unique as you like by adding doodles, patterns, and/or shapes. Color the images any way you like with any tools you like. There are no rules except that you relax, enjoy, and color in a way that feels right to you.

THE MEANING & PURPOSE OF LIFE!

"The meaning of life is to find your gift.
The purpose of life is to give it away."
—Pablo Picasso

THE PSYCHOLOGY OF COLOR!

From my layman's understanding of the meaning of colors, certain colors can evoke certain emotions.

BLUE: centered, calm, hopeful, confidence
GREEN: growth, safety, endurance, calm
ORANGE: energy, happiness, encouragement, excitement
RED: passion, energy, strength, power, determination
YELLOW: joy, energy, cheerfulness
BROWN: stability
PURPLE: power, ambition, creativity, energy
BLACK: power, elegance, mystery
WHITE: light, goodness, safety

So keep that in mind as you color. If you're looking to experience a particular emotion/feeling/mood, you may want to use a particular color to help you get there.

A FEW HELPFUL SUGGESTIONS!

BABY STEPS
I'm a big believer in the power of taking baby steps to get you anywhere you need or want to go, which is why this coloring book is written the way it is. Each day has small-sized activities. They build on each other, one to the next. So feel free to color whichever image you'd like, just know you'll be best served to do the daily activities in order.

NO PERFECTION NEEDED
Do yourself a kindness and make a mistake in this coloring book early on. Scribble on some of the pages. Spill your favorite beverage on the cover. Rip one of the corners off. Color outside the lines. Make this book imperfect so that you'll feel free to be your real, honest self inside the pages. Being real, not being perfect, is what's going to heal you and set you free.

BE HONEST
I'd recommend that you don't show your answers inside this coloring book to anyone. Keep them to yourself for right now until you make it all the way through Day 30. Why? Honesty with yourself is what's going to help you heal and grow. You won't be completely honest if you're worried about someone reading your answers. In fact, what you're likely to do is tweak your responses, edit them, or scratch them out entirely if you're worried about how others might perceive you. So be kind to yourself & let this coloring book be just for you.

BE WILLING & OPEN
The first step to change is to be open & willing to it. You picked up this coloring book because you're struggling in this area of your life. If you want things to be different, well, both you & those things are going to have to change. So be open to experiencing something new & be willing to do the effort to get there.

GIVE YOURSELF PERMISSION
It's hugely important to give yourself permission (whether that's verbally or written) to: do the daily steps in this book, be/have/do/say/believe whatever you need to so that you can heal yourself, give yourself unlimited tries as many times as it takes, believe in your own worth and value, choose to create a life you love because you matter. Whenever you feel like you need someone else's permission to make a choice about your life, you just give that permission to yourself. The only permission you ever need to live your own life is your own.

YOU'RE ON A JOURNEY
It doesn't matter how old you are, how many times you've tried, or how far there is left to go. It's never too late to be the person you want to be. It's okay if you don't know things yet. You're on a journey and you'll figure it out as you go. This coloring book is designed to help you do just that.

BEGIN YOUR DAY WITH A STEP
If at all possible, do your daily step shortly after you wake up. That way, you'll be able to focus on yourself (because you're absolutely worth the time to do that) before your day gets away from you. So grab your favorite beverage. Find a quiet place. Relax and reflect while you're being creative.

IT'S A PRACTICE & A PROCESS
There's no doing this perfectly, and that's okay. You strive for progress. You do the best you can. So show yourself some patience and kindness because self-compassion is what you most need to heal yourself. You will make mistakes, there's just no way around it. Don't ever use any mistake as a reason to give up on yourself. Just circle back around and start again. And know this: every mistake is simply a brand new chance to do it better the next time.

AND FINALLY . . .
Remember (not just for this book but for all of life): you get out what you put in. So make yourself a priority in your own life because: 1. you're absolutely worth the effort and 2. no one else can do it for you. And one last suggestion good both for this book and for all of life: be brave and color outside the lines, that's where freedom lies.

THOSE WHO ARE BRAVE ARE FREE!

"It is not the critic who counts; not the man who points out how the strong man stumbles, or where the doer of deeds could have done them better. The credit belongs to the man who is actually in the arena, whose face is marred by dust and sweat and blood; who strives valiantly; who errs, who comes short again and again, because there is no effort without error and shortcoming; but who does actually strive to do the deeds; who knows great enthusiasms, the great devotions; who spends himself in a worthy cause; who at the best knows in the end the triumph of high achievement, and who at the worst, if he fails, at least fails while daring greatly, so that his place shall never be with those cold and timid souls who neither know victory nor defeat."
— Theodore Roosevelt

Source: excerpt (also known as *The Man In The Arena*) from the speech "Citizenship in a Republic" delivered at The Sorbonne in Paris, France on April 23, 1910.

COLOR TEST PAGE

COLOR TEST PAGE

The only person you are destined to become
is the person you decide to be.
—Ralph Waldo Emerson

1

1. Today, relax.
2. Take a deep breath in through your nose.
3. Hold it for three seconds.
4. Let it out through your mouth.
5. Then pull your shoulders down away from your ears.
6. Repeat five times.
7. Massage your temples & the back of your neck.
8. Repeat often, especially every time you feel like you're not being true to yourself.

2

1. Today, know that you are not alone.
2. You may feel alone. You may feel like everyone else knows exactly who they are, what they want, &/or how best to express their gifts & talents while you flounder around trying to figure it out &/or pretend to be someone else.
3. But know this: one of the main reasons people don't create & live a life they love is because they are not being true to themselves.
4. So don't be so hard on yourself. Instead, remind yourself that you're not alone, that you are in fact in excellent company with the rest of us who aren't/have not been true to ourselves, as often as needed.

3

1. Today, befriend yourself.
2. Know this: you are the closest & best friend you'll ever have. When you aren't true to yourself for any reason, you're not being a friend to yourself; rather, you're telling yourself that you don't like yourself for who you really are. That is an act of self-betrayal. Creating the life you envision for yourself starts with committing today & forever to have your own back *always*. So choose to like yourself as-is, right now, for who you really are.
3. Now write ten positive attributes that you appreciate about yourself. Read that list aloud slowly. Reread when you find yourself hiding your true self.

4

1. Today, give yourself permission *always*.
2. Know this: it doesn't matter if others approve of you or your decisions. What matters most (truly because all your actions stem from what you believe) is whether or not you approve of yourself & the plans that you've made.
3. Know this too: your life belongs to you & you alone; it's entirely up to you to decide who you want to become.
4. So write this & make it your mantra from now on: *the only permission I ever need to become who I most want to be is my own.*

Like yourself as-is.

5
1. Today, listen for your voice of wisdom (also known as your intuition).
2. Know this: your intuition includes both your body (how it feels/reacts) & your mind. It'll *never* tear you down or berate you or harm you. It'll *always* encourage you, strengthen you, & help you grow, even if what it's saying you need to do to be your true self scares you. Your intuition will tell you when you're being true to yourself & when you aren't. *All the answers you need really are inside you.*
3. Stop looking around at anyone/anything else; instead, look inward. Listen for your intuition & write an answer to this: *What does a successful life look like to me?*

Like yourself as-is. Give yourself permission to become who you want to be.

1. Today, trust your intuition.
2. Know this: being true to yourself is what matters most when you make a choice, *any choice.* The only way you'll do that is to trust your intuition & do what it guides you to do. Your intuition is of no use if you won't listen for it & act on what it says.
3. So *every time* you make a choice today & *every day,* pause to listen for your intuition first. (*Do I really want to have/be/do/say this? Does this feel like something I want in my life?*) Then take action accordingly.

Like yourself as-is. Give yourself permission to become who you want to be.

7

1. Today, check your motivation.
2. Know this: the moment your focus becomes trying to please others is the moment that you start living your life for someone else.
3. Write an answer to this: *Just who am I living my own life & meeting my own goals for?* And if the answer is anyone other than yourself, then write an answer to these: *Why am I choosing to do that? Why do I believe that others know what's best for me more than I do?*
4. You know yourself best. So make your own well-being your motivation *every day*.

Like yourself as-is. Give yourself permission to become who you want to be.

8

1. Today, write your creed.
2. Know this: a creed is a personal statement about what deeply matters to you & who you are at your core.
3. Listen for your intuition & write the answers to these: *What ideals do I value? What character traits are most important to me? What are my most strongly held beliefs? What kind of person do I want to be?* (Add any other probing questions you'd like so you can discover those things that deeply matter to you.)

Like yourself as-is. Give yourself permission to become who you want to be.

9

1. Today, hone your creed.
2. Know this: your creed is meant to be a kind of road map, showing you who you want to be as a person & how you want to live your life. It will be much easier for you to use your creed as a guide if it is concise & focused.
3. So read through your answers from Day 8.
4. Now think about each answer, listen for your intuition, & edit down your answers to those ideals/traits/beliefs/characteristics/etcetera that matter the *most* to you. Write that edited version on its own page.

Like yourself as-is. Give yourself permission to become who you want to be.

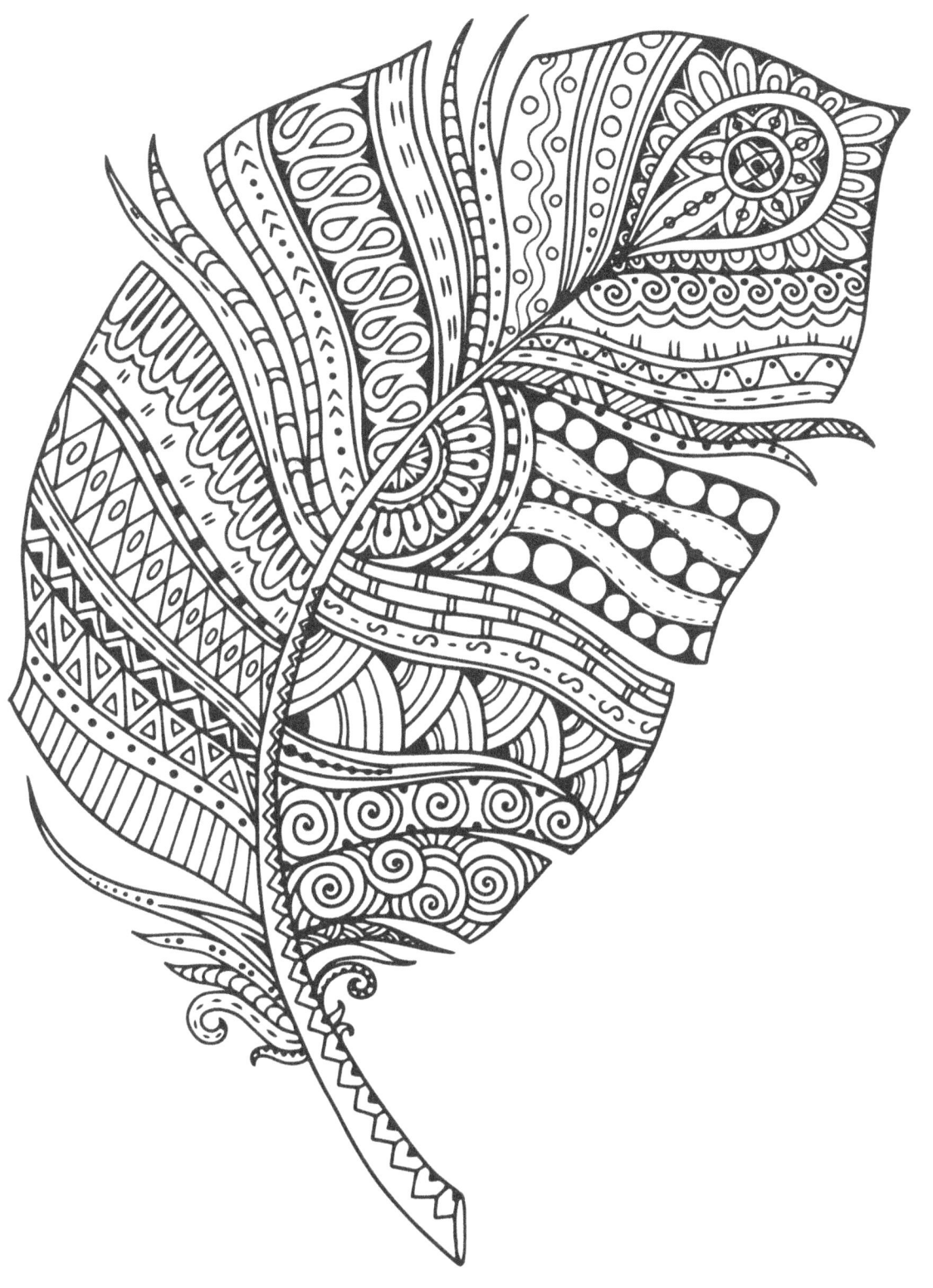

10

1. Today, give up trying to be perfect.
2. Write a list of things you don't like about yourself. Now breathe deeply.
3. Then write an answer to this: *How can I come to peace with those things so I can be happy & enjoy my life right now, this very moment?* (Hint: fix what you can, embrace/let go of what you can't. You'll never be perfect no matter how hard you try; you're human & you make mistakes; so don't set yourself up for failure.)
4. Fix/embrace/let go of your flaws/weaknesses so you're free to be yourself.
5. Now go do something nice for yourself that makes you feel nurtured.

Like yourself as-is. Give yourself permission to become who you want to be.

11

1. Today, find your own true north.
2. Know this: the easiest way to know who you most deeply want to be & what you most deeply want for the whole of your life is to write your own eulogy.
3. So with the end of your life in mind, write the answers to these: *What are the most important things that I want people to know about me & how I lived? What are the most important achievements I made in my life? What do I most want to be remembered for? What do I want my legacy to be when I'm gone?*
4. This is *your* life. It's important that you choose what deeply matters to *you*.

Like yourself as-is. Give yourself permission to become who you want to be.

12

1. Today, hone your own true north.
2. Know this: your eulogy is also meant to be a kind of road map, showing you who you want to be as a person & how you want to live your life. It's meant to guide you as you make choices throughout your life.
3. So read through your answers from Day 11.
4. Now think about each answer, listen for your intuition, & edit your answers to make sure that every answer matters deeply to *you*, then add anything else you may have forgotten that you would want included in your eulogy.

Like yourself as-is. Give yourself permission to become who you want to be.

13

1. Today, practice self-compassion.
2. Know this: if you're not being true to yourself, you're trapped in a mirage/lie & confined to moving through your life as a shimmering figment of your own imagination. Hiding your true self takes an enormous emotional toll on you, starting with decimating your self-esteem.
3. Know this too: discovering who you are is a process & a practice. The more you practice, the easier the process will become.
4. So be kind, gentle, & patient with yourself all day & *every day*.

Like yourself as-is. Give yourself permission to become who you want to be.

14

1. Today, find out what makes you come alive.
2. Listen for your intuition then write the first answer that comes to you (so no overthinking &/or editing) to these: *What activities make me feel the most alive? Where am I & what am I doing when I feel the most happy & fulfilled? What are my passions (things that I love & enjoy)? What makes me feel like this is home &/or where I belong when I do it?*

Like yourself as-is. Give yourself permission to become who you want to be.

15

1. Today, discover your unique gifts & talents.
2. Know this: you are a brilliant genius at something. You were born with a kernel of that genius inside you & your job in this life is to discover what that genius is, to nourish it, to help it (& you) grow, & to share it with the world.
3. Listen for your intuition then write the first answer that comes to you (so no overthinking &/or editing) to these: *What do I love to do &/or lights a spark in me when I do it? What activities do I do that make me lose track of time when I'm doing them? What am I good at? What activities do I naturally gravitate toward?*

Like yourself as-is. Give yourself permission to become who you want to be.

16

1. Today, refuse to compare yourself to anyone else.
2. Know this: you're not growing into someone else, you are growing into yourself. You are on your own journey of self-discovery.
3. Remember: discovering who you truly are is a process & a practice.
4. So don't compare yourself to anyone today (& *every day*).
5. If you find yourself comparing, *gently* remind yourself to stop.

Like yourself as-is. Give yourself permission to become who you want to be.

17

1. Today, define success for yourself.
2. Read through your answers from Days 5, 9, 12, 14, & 15.
3. Using those answers as a reference & keeping in mind that your well-being is your primary motivation now, write down what success looks like to *you* (& not what others might want either for themselves or for you).
4. Listen for your intuition & write an answer to this: *What do I most want to have/be/do/say that would make me believe I am living a successful & fulfilled life?*
5. Be as specific as possible.

Like yourself as-is. Give yourself permission to become who you want to be.

18

1. Today, hone your definition of success.
2. Read through your answer from Day 17.
3. Listen for your intuition then cross off anything that you included because you think/believe that you should want that for your life.
4. Know this: all the should's are about what others want for you. But people come & people go; the only constant guaranteed for your entire life is you.
5. Choose (yes, it's a choice) to let go of any & all thoughts/beliefs of who you should be so that you can become who you actually want to be.

Like yourself as-is. Give yourself permission to become who you want to be.

19

1. Today, know that achieving your definition of success is your life's journey.
2. Rewrite your list from Day 17 so it includes only those things that are not crossed off & reorder that list from most important to you to least important to you in your journey to having a life that is successful for you.
3. Now you know who you want to become, what deeply matters to you, what a successful life would be for you, & in which direction you need to be heading.
4. Armed with that knowledge, do yourself a kindness & say *yes* to choices that will bring you closer to who you really are & what you truly want for your life.

Like yourself as-is. Give yourself permission to become who you want to be.

20

1. Today, honor & respect yourself.
2. Know this: you honor & respect yourself most by trusting yourself.
3. Answer this: *Would I honestly put my life in the hands of someone I didn't trust?* Then know this: your life is already in your hands. It's up to you how you want to live it. To trust yourself, you need to be true to yourself.
4. Now listen for your intuition & write an answer to these: *Why do I believe that hiding my true self &/or pretending to be someone I'm not will fulfill me? What am I trying to gain by not being true to myself?*

Like yourself as-is. Give yourself permission. Define success for yourself.

21

1. Today, find out why.
2. Write a list of what you are afraid will/won't happen if you honor & respect yourself by being true to yourself. Write an answer to these: *What am I trying to avoid by not being true to myself? What do I risk by being my true self?*
3. Listen for your intuition. Be honest. Keep excavating. Write down everything that comes to you. Then find the common thread in your answers & circle it.
4. Take note: that thread is likely your biggest fear & the major reason that you betray yourself & don't show up in the world as your true self.

Like yourself as-is. Give yourself permission. Define success for yourself.

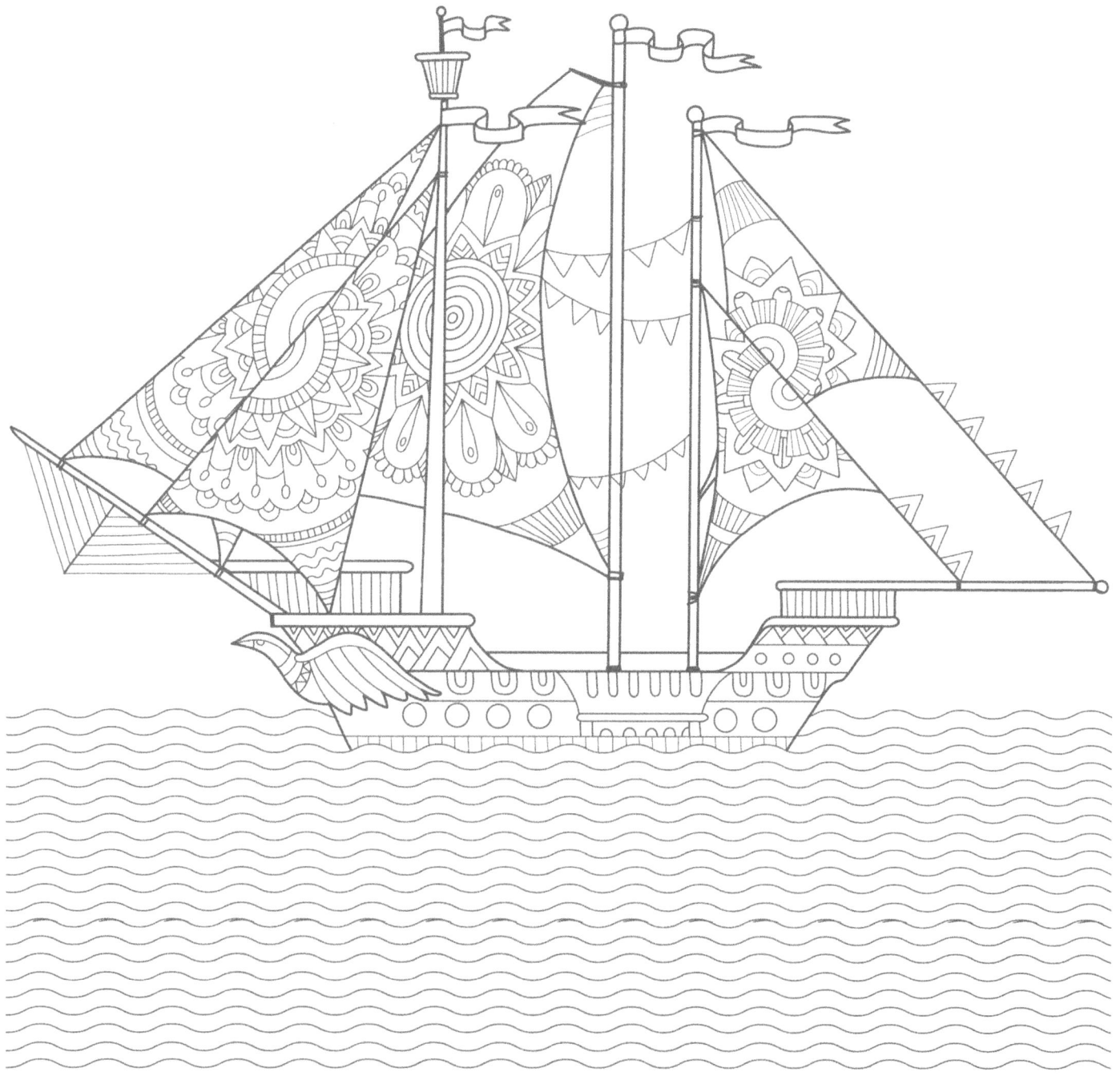

22

1. Today, choose the story you believe.
2. Read through your circled answer (common thread) from Day 21.
3. For that fear, follow it all the way to the end. Write an answer to this: *What's the worst outcome that I imagine will happen?*
4. Now for that same fear, follow it all the way to the end. Listen for your intuition & write an answer to this: *What's the best outcome that I imagine will happen?*
5. Know this: both of those answers are the story you are telling yourself about the outcome. You get to choose which story you want to focus on & believe.

Like yourself as-is. Give yourself permission. Define success for yourself.

23

1. Today, find out what you believe.
2. Know this: you really will live out what you believe.
3. So listen for your intuition & write answers to these: *Do I believe I am worthy of being who I most want to be? Do I believe I am enough as-is with my life the way it is right now? Do I believe I am deserving of good things/success/love/happiness/ etcetera as my true self? Do I believe I matter (& therefore what I do matters) as the person I truly am? Do I believe that I have value as the person I really am? Do I believe I am capable of achieving what I most want for my life?*

Like yourself as-is. Give yourself permission. Define success for yourself.

24

1. Today, change what you believe.
2. Know this: your beliefs either make the walls of the false persona that confines you or they allow you to expand into the authentic person you want to become. Beliefs are simply thoughts you've repeated over & over.
3. So choose (yes, it's a choice) to simply edit any & all beliefs that limit you. Listen for your intuition & write new beliefs that serve to help you stop betraying yourself & instead support you in being true to yourself.
4. Repeat those new beliefs over & over. Let them be what guides you.

Like yourself as-is. Give yourself permission. Define success for yourself.

25

1. Today, honor your preferences.
2. Listen for your intuition & write an answer to these: *What's my particular fashion style? What kind of foods do I love to eat? Where do I feel most at home? What kind of people do I want to surround myself with?* (Add any other probing questions to find *your* unique preferences. Be specific in your answers.)
3. Now you know what you prefer & what feels most true to you. You also know what you have to do to be most authentically yourself. Choose to believe you really can have all your wants/needs/goals/dreams/etcetera.

Like yourself as-is. Give yourself permission. Define success for yourself.

26

1. Today, choose to be happy.
2. Know this: you create the life you're living. You are one-hundred percent responsible for your own happiness.
3. Listen for your intuition & write an answer to these: *Is hiding my true self &/or pretending to be someone other than who I really am making me happy? Do I feel truly alive & excited about my life when I'm not being true to me?*
4. Know this: hiding your gifts/talents, your preferences/beliefs, &/or who you are at your core serves no one, least of all yourself.

Like yourself as-is. Give yourself permission. Define success for yourself.

27

1. Today, be on a mission.
2. Know this: all of us exchange our lives for something; you'll know what that something is by what you devote your time to.
3. Now read through your answers from Days 15 & 19.
4. Listen for your intuition & write a mission statement for your own life that pairs your gifts & talents with your definition of success. Write an active statement as if you're doing it now (so *I am*, not *I will*). Edit until it's short enough that you can remember it. That statement is your strong foundation. Reread it *daily*.

Like yourself as-is. Give yourself permission. Define success for yourself.

28

1. Today, decide who you want to be.
2. Know this: you are with you 24/7. You know yourself better than anyone else. Trust your intuition. Trust that you do know who you are & what you want.
3. Know this too: wherever your heart truly is, that's where your treasure (happiness/fulfillment/joy/money/relationships/etcetera) will be.
4. Don't settle. Don't tell yourself you can't be who you want to be or have what you want to have. Choose to believe you are strong enough & capable enough to become the person you most want to be (because you absolutely are).

Like yourself as-is. Give yourself permission. Define success for yourself.

29

1. Today, relax into yourself & your life.
2. Choose to look at your life as a big experiment. You're on a journey to see what works for you & what doesn't. Choose to remove the pressure, stress, & hurry so you can discover yourself & find out what makes *you* come alive.
3. Go as slowly as you like. It doesn't matter *in the least* how slowly you go as long as you keep moving & you don't stop.

Like yourself as-is. Give yourself permission. Define success for yourself.

30

1. Today, celebrate!
2. Be proud of yourself for how far you've come.
3. Write down your successes & victories (big or small).
4. Do something nice for yourself (like a prize for a job well done).
5. Go & enjoy your life!

Like yourself as-is. Give yourself permission. Define success for yourself.

ABOUT THE AUTHOR!

This book was born out of Shelli Johnson's own struggle with being herself. She wanted and needed to heal herself. She wanted and needed practical and easy steps she could take to stop living the life others wanted her to live and instead to step out and live a life that was true to herself. So she simply wrote the book she needed to read. Every day, she does her best to cut herself some slack & practice progress, not perfection.

Shelli's also an award-winning journalist (sports reporting), novelist (grand prize winner), and blogger (shellijohnson.com/blog). She's a truck owner, horse rider, photographer, yoga enthusiast, and slow-cooker fan (shellijohnson.com/recipes). Find out more at: shellijohnson.com/about

Find out about Shelli's other books at:
shellijohnson.com/books

GET YOUR FREE STUFF!

Visit: shellijohnson.com/signup
Opt-in for the newsletter to keep in touch.
Get a free bookmark to color.

ACKNOWLEDGMENTS!

My sincere thanks to people who make my days brighter:
Rollin Johnson
Heather Porazzo

Disclosures and Disclaimers

This book is published in print format. All trademarks and service marks are the properties of their respective owners. All references to these properties are made solely for editorial purposes. Except for marks actually owned by the Author or the Publisher, no commercial claims are made to their use, and neither the Author nor the Publisher is affiliated with such marks in any way.

Unless otherwise expressly noted, none of the individuals or business entities mentioned herein has endorsed the contents of this book.

Limits of Liability & Disclaimers of Warranties

Because this book is a general educational information product, it is not a substitute for professional advice on the topics discussed in it.

The materials in this book are provided "as is" and without warranties of any kind either express or implied. The Author and the Publisher disclaim all warranties, express or implied, including, but not limited to, implied warranties of merchantability and fitness for a particular purpose. The Author and the Publisher do not warrant that defects will be corrected. The Author does not warrant or make any representations regarding the use or the results of the use of the materials in this book in terms of their correctness, accuracy, reliability, or otherwise. Applicable law may not allow the exclusion of implied warranties, so the above exclusion may not apply to you.

Under no circumstances, including, but not limited to, negligence, shall the Author or the Publisher be liable for any special or consequential damages that result from the use of, or the inability to use this book, even if the Author, the Publisher, or an authorized representative has been advised of the possibility of such damages. Applicable law may not allow the limitation or exclusion of liability or incidental or consequential damages, so the above limitation or exclusion may not apply to you. In no event shall the Author or Publisher total liability to you for all damages, losses, and causes of action (whether in contract, tort, including but not limited to, negligence or otherwise) exceed the amount paid by you, if any, for this book.

You agree to hold the Author and the Publisher of this book, principals, agents, affiliates, and employees harmless from any and all liability for all claims for damages due to injuries, including attorney fees and costs, incurred by you or caused to third parties by you, arising out of the products, services, and activities discussed in this book, excepting only claims for gross negligence or intentional tort.

You agree that any and all claims for gross negligence or intentional tort shall be settled solely by confidential binding arbitration per the American Arbitration Association's commercial arbitration rules. Your claim cannot be aggregated with third party claims. All arbitration must occur in the municipality where the Author's principal place of business is located. Arbitration fees and costs shall be split equally, and you are solely responsible for your own lawyer fees.

Facts and information are believed to be accurate at the time they were placed in this book. All data provided in this book is to be used for information purposes only. The information contained within is not intended to provide specific legal, financial, tax, physical or mental health advice, or any other advice whatsoever, for any individual or company and should not be relied upon in that regard. The services described are only offered in jurisdictions where they may be legally offered. Information provided is not all-inclusive, and is limited to information that is made available and such information should not be relied upon as all-inclusive or accurate.

For more information about this policy, please contact the Author at the website address listed in the Copyright Notice at the front of this book.

IF YOU DO NOT AGREE WITH THESE TERMS AND EXPRESS CONDITIONS, DO NOT READ THIS BOOK. YOUR USE OF THIS BOOK, INCLUDING PRODUCTS, SERVICES, AND ANY PARTICIPATION IN ACTIVITIES MENTIONED IN THIS BOOK, MEAN THAT YOU ARE AGREEING TO BE LEGALLY BOUND BY THESE TERMS.

Affiliate Compensation & Material Connections Disclosure

This book may contain references to websites and information created and maintained by other individuals and organizations. The Author and the Publisher do not control or guarantee the accuracy, completeness, relevance, or timeliness of any information or privacy policies posted on these websites.

You should assume that all references to products and services in this book are made because material connections exist between the Author or Publisher and the providers of the mentioned products and services ("Provider"). You should also assume that all website links within this book are affiliate links for (a) the Author, (b) the Publisher, or (c) someone else who is an affiliate for the mentioned products and services (individually and collectively, the "Affiliate").

The Affiliate recommends products and services in this book based in part on a good faith belief that the purchase of such products or services will help readers in general.

The Affiliate has this good faith belief because (a) the Affiliate has tried the product or service mentioned prior to recommending it or (b) the Affiliate has researched the reputation of the Provider and has made the decision to recommend the Provider's products or services based on the Provider's history of providing these or other products or services.

The representations made by the Affiliate about products and services reflect the Affiliate's honest opinion based upon the facts known to the Affiliate at the time this book was published.

Because there is a material connection between the Affiliate and Providers of products or services mentioned in this book, you should always assume that the Affiliate may be biased because of the Affiliate's relationship with a Provider and/or because the Affiliate has received or will receive something of value from a Provider.

Perform your own due diligence before purchasing a product or service mentioned in this book.

The type of compensation received by the Affiliate may vary. In some instances, the Affiliate may receive complimentary products (such as a review copy), services, or money from a Provider prior to mentioning the Provider's products or services in this book.

In addition, the Affiliate may receive a monetary commission or non-monetary compensation when you take action by using a website link within in this book. This includes, but is not limited to, when you purchase a product or service from a Provider after going to a website link contained in this book.

Health Disclaimers

As an express condition to reading to this book, you understand and agree to the following terms.

This book is a general educational health-related information product. This book does not contain medical advice.

The book's content is not a substitute for direct, personal, professional medical care and diagnosis. None of the exercises or treatments (including products and services) mentioned in this book should be performed or otherwise used without prior approval from your physician or other qualified professional health care provider.

There may be risks associated with participating in activities or using products and services mentioned in this book for people in poor health or with pre-existing physical or mental health conditions.

Because these risks exist, you will not use such products or participate in such activities if you are in poor health or have a pre-existing mental or physical condition. If you choose to participate in these risks, you do so of your own free will and accord, knowingly and voluntarily assuming all risks associated with such activities.

Earnings & Income Disclaimers
No Earnings Projections, Promises or Representations

For purposes of these disclaimers, the term "Author" refers individually and collectively to the author of this book and to the affiliate (if any) whose affiliate hyperlinks are referenced in this book.

You recognize and agree that the Author and the Publisher have made no implications, warranties, promises, suggestions, projections, representations or guarantees whatsoever to you about future prospects or earnings, or that you will earn any money, with respect to your purchase of this book, and that the Author and the Publisher have not authorized any such projection, promise, or representation by others.

Any earnings or income statements, or any earnings or income examples, are only estimates of what you might earn. There is no assurance you will do as well as stated in any examples. If you rely upon any figures provided, you must accept the entire risk of not doing as well as the information provided. This applies whether the earnings or income examples are monetary in nature or pertain to advertising credits which may be earned (whether such credits are convertible to cash or not).

There is no assurance that any prior successes or past results as to earnings or income (whether monetary or advertising credits, whether convertible to cash or not) will apply, nor can any prior successes be used, as an indication of your future success or results from any of the information, content, or strategies. Any and all claims or representations as to income or earnings (whether monetary or advertising credits, whether convertible to cash or not) are not to be considered as "average earnings".

Testimonials & Examples

Testimonials and examples in this book are exceptional results, do not reflect the typical purchaser's experience, do not apply to the average person and are not intended to represent or guarantee that anyone will achieve the same or similar results. Where specific income or earnings (whether monetary or advertising credits, whether convertible to cash or not), figures are used and attributed to a specific individual or business, that individual or business has earned that amount. There is no assurance that you will do as well using the same information or strategies. If you rely on the specific income or earnings figures used, you must accept all the risk of not doing as well. The described experiences are atypical. Your financial results are likely to differ from those described in the testimonials.

The Economy

The economy, where you do business, on a national and even worldwide scale, creates additional uncertainty and economic risk. An economic recession or depression might negatively affect your results.

Your Success or Lack of It

Your success in using the information or strategies provided in this book depends on a variety of factors. The Author and the Publisher have no way of knowing how well you will do because they do not know you, your background, your work ethic, your dedication, your motivation, your desire, or your business skills or practices. Therefore, neither the Author nor the Publisher guarantees or implies that you will get rich, that you will do as well, or that you will have any earnings (whether monetary or advertising credits, whether convertible to cash or not), at all.

Businesses and earnings derived therefrom involve unknown risks and are not suitable for everyone. You may not rely on any information presented in this book or otherwise provided by the Author or the Publisher, unless you do so with the knowledge and understanding that you can experience significant losses (including, but not limited to, the loss of any monies paid to purchase this book and/or any monies spent setting up, operating, and/or marketing your business activities, and further, that you may have no earnings at all (whether monetary or advertising credits, whether convertible to cash or not).

Forward-Looking Statements

Materials in this book may contain information that includes or is based upon forward-looking statements within the meaning of the Securities Litigation Reform Act of 1995. Forward-looking statements give the Author's expectations or forecasts of future events. You can identify these statements by the fact that they do not relate strictly to historical or current facts. They use words such as "anticipate," "estimate," "expect," "project," "intend," "plan," "believe," and other words and terms of similar meaning in connection with a description of potential earnings or financial performance.

Any and all forward looking statements here or on any materials in this book are intended to express an opinion of earnings potential. Many factors will be important in determining your actual results and no guarantees are made that you will achieve results similar to the Author or anybody else. In fact, no guarantees are made that you will achieve any results from applying the Author's ideas, strategies, and tactics found in this book.

Purchase Price

Although the Publisher believes the price is fair for the value that you receive, you understand and agree that the purchase price for this book has been arbitrarily set by the Publisher or the vendor who sold you this book. This price bears no relationship to objective standards.

Due Diligence

You are advised to do your own due diligence when it comes to making any decisions. Use caution and seek the advice of qualified professionals before acting upon the contents of this book or any other information. You shall not consider any examples, documents, or other content in this book or otherwise provided by the Author or Publisher to be the equivalent of professional advice.

The Author and the Publisher assume no responsibility for any losses or damages resulting from your use of any link, information, or opportunity contained in this book or within any other information disclosed by the Author or the Publisher in any form whatsoever.

YOU SHOULD ALWAYS CONDUCT YOUR OWN INVESTIGATION (PERFORM DUE DILIGENCE)
BEFORE BUYING PRODUCTS OR SERVICES FROM ANYONE. THIS INCLUDES PRODUCTS AND SERVICES
SOLD VIA WEBSITE LINKS REFERENCED IN THIS BOOK.

www.ingramcontent.com/pod-product-compliance
Lightning Source LLC
Chambersburg PA
CBHW081351080526
44588CB00016B/2454